2023 Travel Guide To Santo Domingo(Dominican Republic)

The Ultimate travel guide to Santo Domingo, Discover the Tropical Paradise Of Dominican Republic with Well Planned perfect itinerary.

Steven S. Bender

All right reserved.No part of this publication may be reduced,
distributed,or transmitted in any form or by any means,
including photocopying, recording,or any other electronic or
or mechanical methods, without the prior written permission
of the publisher, except in the case of brief quotations embodied
in critical reviews and certain other non-commercial uses
permitted by copyright law.
Copyright @Steven S.Bender ,2023

Table Of Content
Introduction
Why Go To Santo Domingo
Entry Requirements
E-TICKET
7 Best Hotels In Santo Domingo
Best Time To Visit Santo Domingo
Unmissable Things to Do in Santo Domingo – Dominican Republic's Capital
6 Best Santo Domingo Beaches
How to Save Money in Santo Domingo
Culture & Customs
10 Great Restaurants in Santo Domingo
Getting Around Santo Domingo
Plan Your Dominican Republic Honeymoon
Conclusion

Introduction

The Dominican Republic, a republic in the West Indies that encompasses the eastern two-thirds of Hispaniola, is the second biggest island of the Greater Antilles group in the Caribbean Sea. Haiti, likewise an independent republic, occupies the western portion of the island.

The Dominican Republic's coasts are washed by the Caribbean to the south and the Atlantic Ocean to the north. Between the eastern edge of the island and Puerto Rico runs the Mona Passage, a strait approximately 80 miles (130 km) wide. The Turks and Caicos Islands are situated around 90 miles (145 km) to the north, while Colombia is about 300 miles (500 km) to the south. The republic's territory, which includes such surrounding islands as Saona, Beata, and Catalina, is nearly half the size of Portugal. The national capital is Santo Domingo, on the southern coast.

The Dominican Republic has much in common with the nations of Latin America (with which it is commonly classified), and some authors have referred to the country as a microcosm of that area.

Dominicans have experienced political and civil disorder, ethnic tensions, export-oriented booms and busts, and long periods of military rule, including a Haitian occupation (1822–44), the oppressive dictatorship of Rafael Trujillo (1930–61), and military interventions by the United States (1916–24 and 1965–66). (1916–24 and 1965–66).

However, the nation's woes have paled in contrast with those of neighboring Haiti.

The two nations have long been considered crucial because of their closeness to the United States and their placement on vital maritime routes leading to the Caribbean and the Panama Canal.

Why Go To Santo Domingo

Christopher Columbus attempted to settle in the "New World" multiple times before getting it right. The first and second efforts, La Navidad (in Haiti) and La Isabela (near Puerto Plata), were afflicted by fire and sickness.

It wasn't until the third trip, on a different shore of Hispaniola, that he and his men refined the formula. To this day, Santo Domingo is still a bustling, flourishing metropolis and operates as both the capital city of the Dominican Republic and the biggest city in the Caribbean by population. But it's also so much more:

The sounds of merengue, bachata, and salsa flowing from a Malecón nightclub or the fragrance of conch gratinée wafting from a romantic café in Zona Colonial.

Due to its history, it's also a city of superlatives: there you'll discover the earliest church (Catedral Primada de América), the first fortress (Fortaleza Ozama), and the oldest street (Calle Las Damas) in the Americas. This is the actual Santo Domingo.

Entry Requirements

As of April 23, 2022, all passengers and crew members do not need to submit a COVID-19 Vaccination Card, PCR, or antigen test to enter the Dominican Republic to attend tourist areas, or any enterprises or to get services such as excursions.

Random COVID-19 testing for passengers and personnel upon arrival in the Dominican Republic will no longer be undertaken. However, when needed, random testing activities may be done. Passengers who submit their Vaccination Cards will be excused from random testing.

Passports: All foreign nationals who visit the Dominican Republic, primarily for tourist reasons, must have a valid passport throughout their stay and exit from the country. This special measure is active until April 30, 2023.

EXCEPTIONS TO THE VALIDITY OF PASSPORTS

Subject to reciprocity, the following foreigners are exempt:

- 1. Diplomatic officers and consular officials accredited in the Dominican Republic, as well as other members of permanent or special diplomatic missions and consular posts and their family members who, under the rules of International Law, are exempt from the obligations related to obtaining a migratory category of entry;

- 2. Representatives and delegates, as well as the other members and their families of the permanent Missions or of the Delegations before the Intergovernmental Organizations with headquarters in the Dominican Republic or in International Conferences that are celebrated in it;

- 3. Officials assigned to International and Intergovernmental Organizations with headquarters in the Dominican Republic and their family members, as well as holders of Dominican diplomatic and official visas.

Under the discretionary power granted by the Law to the Director General of Immigration, he may authorize the entry into the country of foreigners of United States citizens who do not meet the requirements outlined in the Law and its regulations, when there are exceptional reasons for a humanitarian nature, public interest or compliance with commitments undertaken by the Dominican Republic. Each permission is a case in point and, accordingly, does not represent a binding reference or precedent.

Based on the ever-changing nature of the COVID-19 virus, we suggest contacting your airline or travel agency directly to discuss any procedures that may apply to your nation.

As needed, we also suggest consulting the Overseas Air Transport Association (IATA) for any revisions to international markets and their related processes. IATA cannot guarantee its correctness and can take no duty for any errors or omissions.

E-TICKET

All international and Dominican passengers entering or departing the Dominican Republic on commercial flights must complete the free electronic entrance and departure form, which combines the Traveler's Health Affidavit, Customs Declaration, and International Embarkation/Disembarkation forms.

Current Measures By The Government Of The Dominican Republic

As of February 16, 2022, all restrictive measures imposed by COVID-19 are suspended, and it will be up to each person to adopt his or her actions to preserve his or her health, responsibly, but without limits.

Measures such as the wearing of face masks, and the presentation of vaccination certificates for admission to places of public use or limits in public areas are the responsibility of each person.

As a consequence of our severe safety precautions and excellent vaccination campaign, today, hotel occupancy has grown to 100%, further reinforcing the Dominican Republic as a global model of tourism recovery throughout the epidemic.

100% of the Tourism sector staff (hotels, airports, restaurants, transportation, etc.) have been vaccinated with two doses, and are in the process of getting vaccinated with a third dosage of the vaccine against COVID-19.

With this immunization program, we will continue to enhance the safety and health of all individuals who work in the industry to likewise ensure the safety and health of all visitors that visit us. The hotels, restaurants, and businesses will continue to work hand in hand with the authorities.

The Dominican Republic has a solid healthcare system that has been able to promptly diagnose instances of COVID-19 in the nation.

For more information about the coronavirus in the Dominican Republic, please visit the Ministry of Public Health's website or download the COVID-RD mobile phone application, available on the App Store and Google Play, that works as a passport in which, through a QR code, visitors can report their condition and access many services and information.

For MITUR, the well-being and safety of tourists remain a priority, thus it will continue to work in conjunction with the other necessary agencies to further reinforce the country's preventative measures against coronavirus.

World Tourism Organization (UNWTO) recognition

On May 9, 2022, the World Tourism Organization (UNWTO) acknowledged the Dominican Republic as the number one nation in the world in tourism recovery. The Dominican tourism model stands out for producing the most effective recovery in the sector, hitting record levels in visitor arrivals.

The success of the recovery is attributed to the Dominican Government and the pillars of innovation, entrepreneurship, education, and new destinations, which are the basis for the cooperative effort between the public and private sectors, which jointly ensure the guarantees and health protocols to guarantee safe tourism.

On January 18, 2022, the World Tourism Organization (UNWTO) acknowledged the Dominican Republic for its excellent recovery in the tourism sector and its effective administration of sanitary regulations in the country's diverse tourist attractions.

The UNWTO emphasized the management and sanitary measures used in the Dominican Republic to assure safe tourism, thereby producing the most effective recovery of the sector in the whole area, reaching record levels in visitor arrivals.

The success of the recovery is thanks to the collaborative effort of the public and commercial sectors, who continue to work hand in hand with the Association of Hotels and Tourism (ASONAHORES) (ASONAHORES).

The Dominican Republic is the only destination in the area where 100% of the personnel in the tourism sector are completely vaccinated with two doses, and it has the lowest incidence rate of contagion in the tourist poles, making the country a safe destination for travel.

Thanks to its recovery, the Dominican Republic has become a tourist reference in the area.

7 Best Hotels In Santo Domingo

1. JW Marriott Hotel Santo Domingo
This JW Marriott outpost provides modern luxury in Santo Domingo's upscale suburb of Piantini, less than 2 miles southwest of the city center. Travelers with a fondness for the better things in life will particularly enjoy the hotel's position feet from the luxury BlueMall, which boasts boutiques like Cartier, Zara, and Louis Vuitton.

But customers say the JW Marriott Hotel Santo Domingo is also a perfect site for business travelers because of its central location and multiple business services and facilities, not to mention the considerable desk space in the rooms. Accommodations at this Marriott are regarded as comfy and sophisticated, with beige and white color palettes, leather headboards, and sleek wood furniture. Amenities are numerous. In the rooms, visitors are greeted with pillow-top mattresses, marble baths, minifridges, coffee machines, and complimentary bottled water. Visitors may employ the hotel's grocery shopping service, work up a sweat in the fitness facility, take a plunge in the rooftop infinity pool, or wine and dine at the Vertygo 101 - Lounge & Bar or the Winston's Grill & Patio.

But critics believe the highlight of the JW Marriot Hotel Santo Domingo is its exceptional customer service, with many guests claiming the personnel made them feel perfectly at home. What's more, Marriott Bonvoy members may earn or spend points here for added rewards.

2. Billini Hotel, Historic Luxury
Those wishing to experience Santo Domingo's ancient charm can try laying down at the Billini Hotel.

This boutique facility (which falls inside the city's UNESCO World Heritage-listed Zona Colonial) highlights features of the region's history, such as brick archways and ancient exposed walls in some of the guest rooms. But don't let its old-world setting mislead you.

The Billini Hotel offers many contemporary conveniences, too. To start, all 24 suites have benefits like flat-screen smart TVs, coffee machines, and complimentary wireless internet access. Recent guests notably praised the hotel's old-meets-new ambiance and its friendly staff, however, some thought the complimentary daily breakfast lacked selections.

Outside of your modest lodgings, you'll discover attractions like a spa, three restaurants, a café, a wine cellar, a business center, and an outdoor pool. Past visitors are enthused about the rooftop pool's perspectives, which include a beautiful view of La Regina Angelorum, one of the earliest churches founded in the New World.

3. El Embajador, a Royal Hideaway Hotel

Surrounded by the hustle and bustle of Santo Domingo's business sector, El Embajador offers visitors both an urban ambiance and ideal beach access.

Recent guests hailed the hotel as exquisite, noting the historical design highlights like crystal chandeliers in the lobby and antique furniture in the suites. However, several prior guests regarded the property's location as more suitable for business travelers and couples who tied the knot than for sightseers.

Whether you're staying here for work or enjoyment, you'll have access to amenities including three restaurants (one of which is dedicated exclusively for Royal Level guests), two bars, a spa, a business center, a casino, and two pools. Plus, all suites feature complimentary Wi-Fi access, smart TVs, and iHome clock radios, among other perks.

4. Renaissance Santo Domingo Jaragua Hotel & Casino

Situated on the busy Malecon, the Marriott-affiliated Renaissance Santo Domingo Jaragua Hotel & Casino provides a convenient location for guests wishing to experience Santo Domingo's modern area. Visitors love the new design and feel the hotel provides for a pleasant stay.

Rooms include comfortable beds, Aveda toiletries, and, in select rooms, views of the Caribbean Sea. But with all of the other conveniences, you may not need to spend much time in your quarters.

Travellers say the pool is spacious, well-maintained, and directly across the street from the coast. For a bit extra pampering, go to the spa. Or, if you're inclined to try Lady Luck, check out the on-site casino. After you work up an appetite, get a snack at one of the hotel's two restaurants, Luna Bar & Restaurant and Sol Pool Lounge & Restaurant.

The hotel also has a coffee shop with handcrafted gelato for those with sweet tooths. Recent visitors' lone criticism was the sometimes mediocre customer service. However, if you're a Marriott Bonvoy member, you may earn or redeem points here.

5. Sheraton Santo Domingo Hotel
If you're searching for something basic and comfy for your holiday (not to mention economical), then the Sheraton Santo Domingo Hotel may be the ideal choice.

The hotel's 245 guest rooms are furnished in neutral color palettes and include Sheraton Sweet Sleeper mattresses, flat-screen TVs, minibars, and an adequate work area.

Outside the rooms, the hotel features a well-equipped fitness facility, with a business center and an outdoor pool. But what sticks out about this Sheraton hotel is its location. The hotel is adjacent to the city's famous Zona Colonial, the business sector, and the Don Diego cruise port.

Not only that but the hotel is located across the street from the ocean, which means visitors may enjoy water views from upgraded suites' floor-to-ceiling windows or balconies. In addition to having a fantastic location, customers appreciate the property's top-notch customer service, with many claiming that the staff went out of their way to make their stay exceptional.

Others delight in the food offered at the globally oriented Cafe Casabe Restaurant, the sushi venue, and the pool restaurant. However, a few travelers did report minor accommodation difficulties including faulty air-conditioning equipment and insufficient water pressure in their showers. Remember, this facility is part of the Marriott hotel family, so Marriott Bonvoy members may earn or spend points while staying here.

6. Catalonia Santo Domingo
Catalonia Santo Domingo attracts both business and leisure tourists. This Santo Domingo hotel provides over 12,000 square feet of conference space, a business center, and free Wi-Fi access, so your only excuse for a slip in productivity is the surrounding beach.

If you don't have deadlines to worry about, spend some time by the pool or drinking drinks at one of two bars. Recent customers commended the clean and large (although old) guest rooms, equipped with flat-screen TVs, minibars, work tables, and coffee machines. However, some prior tourists had conflicting emotions about the property's location. While some enjoyed its closeness to the Malecon, others wished it had more eateries within walking distance and was closer to key attractions like Zona Colonial. If you'd prefer to eat on-site, go to the Sea Blue Breakfast for buffet-style breakfasts, Filigrana Restaurant for Dominican-inspired lunches and evenings, or Five Hundred Snack Bar for pizzas, tapas, and more.

7. Crowne Plaza Santo Domingo

With its superb position along the Malecón, only a mile southwest of Zona Colonial, this Crowne Plaza outpost is a wonderful home base for exploring Santo Domingo.

Previous visitors liked the ocean views from the guest rooms, which also come equipped with coffee machines, minibars, free Wi-Fi access, and flat-screen TVs. If you're able to separate from your snug quarters, the Crowne Plaza Santo Domingo does provide various options to enjoy the warm weather, including a pool and jacuzzi. Plus, the on-site spa and casino enable you to kick back and decompress. For a more vibrant ambiance, travel to Level 1 for a beverage and live nightly music or get a bite to eat at the pool bar, the lobby's informal Kaffetto's cafe, or the American-focused Nabu Restaurant.

Though most prior guests loved the property's amenities, several advised that the restaurant menus are restricted and that the on-site gym and pool are modest. But keep in mind, members of the IHG Rewards Club program may earn or spend points for stays here.

Best Time To Visit Santo Domingo

The ideal time to visit Santo Domingo is between November and March. That's when this city has its greatest beach weather, even if there aren't many fantastic beaches to enjoy it on.

April to July is also a nice time to come, but you should avoid this location at all costs during the hurricane season, which runs from August to October.

Whenever you arrive, you'll find the hotel costs are pleasant; even the top establishments have rooms available for less than $150 a night.

April-July

This is an excellent season for Santo Domingo's yearly events — like the thrilling Merengue Festival or the studious International Book Fair — and you'll also get to enjoy some of the Dominican Republic's nicest weather — temperatures should settle somewhere between the mid-70s and low 90s.

Key Events:

International Book Fair (May) (May)
Merengue Festival (July-August) (July-August)

August-October

Do you enjoy the rain? '
Cause you'll see lots of it this time of year. And given what a vast walking town this is, you're best off keeping away during the heat. There's also the danger of hurricanes.

Key Events:

Merengue Festival (July-August) (July-August)
Puerto Plata Festival (October) (October)
November-March
From late autumn through winter, the typical highs are in the mid-80s; lows are in the high 60s.

In other words, it's great weather for walking around the Malecón. You could observe a minor bump in travelers around March for spring break, but it'll scarcely be visible. Most travelers opt to lodge near the more magnificent shorelines of Punta Cana and Puerto Plata. If you are hoping to save a little money on a wintertime vacation to the DR, consider visiting this city instead.

Key Events:

Santo Domingo Colonial Fest (November) (November)
Santo Domingo Carnival (February-March) (February-March)

Unmissable Things to Do in Santo Domingo – Dominican Republic's Capital

The capital city of the Dominican Republic, Santo Domingo is sometimes neglected by vacationers visiting the island who prefer Dominican beach towns or resort vacations.

But Santo Domingo, formerly the capital of the Hispanic Americas, is one of the most intriguing and thrilling places to visit! This city is alive in social movements, culture, food, nightlife, and events virtually every day. There are loads of things to do in Santo Domingo for every tourist!

And with over one million residents residing in the city, you'll find yourself seeing Dominicans from every walk of life, from farmers to community leaders to the pope (Dominican slang for preppy hipsters) (Dominican slang for preppy hipsters). So if you're thinking about things to do in Santo Domingo... Well, here's a little bit of everything for everyone in this dynamic city. Santo Domingo is also the ideal launching pad for numerous day and side excursions, making it an opportune spot to stop by and recuperate in between your adventures across the Dominican Republic.

1. Visit La Zona Colonial
If you can only do one thing while in Santo Domingo, then let it be this. Hands down. La Zona Colonial is the old colonial core of the city.

Here you may spend days discovering Santo Domingo's top things to see and see. This is also one of the greatest destinations to visit in the Dominican Republic for cultural events, social movements, art galleries, museums, nightlife, and fashionable restaurants.

If you're afraid that this is an area solely for visitors or touristy stuff, it's a neighborhood for both residents and tourists.

You'll discover local artists, local theatre, local community centers, local LGBT pubs, and much more! So if you appreciate history and culture — La Zona Colonial is the place to go in Santo Domingo.

A majority of the items discussed in this essay are in la Zona Colonial. But here is a brief rundown of the best historic streets/plazas you can't miss out on in la Zona Colonial:

Catching a peek at the oldest church in the Americas (built on a holy indigenous site, ugh) (built over a sacred indigenous site, yikes)
Strolling around the old Las Damas Street
People-watch at Parque Colon
Get a drink at one of the restaurants in Plaza de Espana/Armas like Pat'e Palo.

Stroll through the old street of El Conde
Casa Quien Art Gallery Centro Cultural Español: Cultural venue financed by the Spanish embassy includes art exhibitions, films, concerts, and more.

2. Microteatro: 15-Minute Plays about Dominican Life

Microteatro Santo Domingo is a unique theatre idea 15-minute play by Dominican actors/writers on local Dominican life, culture, love, and relationships.

It's in a small and occasionally participatory setting frequently with just you and a dozen other onlookers + the actors. The plays I've seen here have been humorous, and thought-provoking, and vary in taste and presentation.

The Microteatro facility is in a lovely colonial structure and as such features an open-air patio where you may dine and drink. This is one of the greatest evenings out in Santo Domingo with friends or family. Eat, drink, and watch 4 different 15-minute plays in between.

You may purchase your tickets there shortly before the event, but, it typically gets sold out so it's advisable to there early.

3. Quinta Dominica
Housed in a 1500s Spanish villa, this cultural center presents many programs about history and tradition. I originally came here for a conversation about the history of slavery in the Dominican Republic.

Afterward, I got to converse, argue, and engage with the speaker and other participants. There is an art museum with rotating exhibitions before you reach the magnificent outdoor courtyard area surrounded by towering mango trees. If you arrive on the day, do not pass up on freshly produced mango juice. The ideal delicacy to savor when meeting up with friends or as a break between your Zona Colonial explorations.

4. El Museo de la Resistencia

A visit to this museum is a terrific chance to educate yourself on the history around you, to better contextualize your experience around the nation, and to support a worthy cause. This museum largely celebrates people who have struggled against persecution, such as the legendary dictatorship of Rafael Trujillo. The museum comprises artwork, movies, narratives, images, and more.

You may spend hours here. But please know that it is only in Spanish nonetheless, you might hire a local guide to translate for you. There is also a stunning outdoor colonial courtyard positioned between displays.

5. Amber Museum

Amber is tree resin "gemstones" from ~20 million years ago! Inside, you may discover relics of extinct flora and creatures. But Dominican amber is much more remarkable. Come to this museum to find out why.

This Santo Domingo site is a must-visit for gemstone/geology aficionados!

While I was there, I got to meet the Dominican owner, who gave me a tour of the museum. You could see that the family has a great interest in geology and Dominican ancestry. His daughter is also Joarla Caridad, who crafts wonderful artisan larimar and amber jewelry.

6. Museo de las Casas Reales

The Museum of the Royal Houses gives a peek into the history and cultural legacy of the Dominican Republic, beginning with Christoper Columbus' invasion. This edifice was previously the palace of the governor of Santo Domingo (one step below the Queen of Spain) (one step below the Queen of Spain).

It was the earliest and oldest headquarters of Spain's colonization of the Americas. It's crucial to emphasize that many museums in Latin America still concentrate on the viewpoint of the European colonizer.

7. Los Tres Ojos National Park & Open Caves Systems

The Dominican Republic's Three Eyes National Park is a natural reserve and open-air limestone cave system with a succession of crystal clear lakes known as the "eyes." Located in Santo Domingo, approximately 10 minutes by vehicle from the famed Colonial Zone, the park gives a delightful relief from the rush and bustle of the bustling city. Along with a guided tour, these spectacular open-water caverns also give deeper insights into the pre-colonial and ancestral beginnings of the Dominican Republic.

8. Mamey Libreria + La Ximena

This was a Santo Domingo highlight experience for people wanting a little of everything in one area. Mamey Liberia formerly had art galleries, a bookshop, an independent theatre in the rear, and a café where you may get beverages or food.

Now it's just the bookshop that remains (with some amazing Dominican-related books), a new cigar room, and a new bar/restaurant area. It has new proprietors who have converted it from a cultural center to it seeming like more of a nightlife area named Ximena. But it's still fresh. So let's see.

Cultural activities (concerts and gatherings) also used to take place here, so maybe Ximena will continue that legacy; be on the watch through their Instagram.

Regardless of the current alterations, Mamey was the previous colonial house of Dominican historian Emilio Rodriguez Demorizi. It continues to be embellished with a Spanish/Moorish-influenced style and little courtyards with plants.

9. Larimar Museum

Larimar is one of the world's rarest semi-precious stones, unique solely to the Dominican Republic and only discovered in one mine in the province of Barahona. Its delicate cyan-blue hue perfectly suits the ocean of its coastlines well.

This Larimar museum is little but incredibly intriguing and pleasant to browse around. It is free and stands above a Larimar shop, so feel free to browse around and go upstairs to access the museum. If you appreciate geology, and interesting rocks/gemstones, this tiny museum is a must-visit! It's a simple visit and takes approximately 20-45 minutes to finish.

10. Ride El Teleferico

For less than .50 cents USD you may ride the spotlessly clean metro in Santo Domingo and then receive a free connection to the teleférico (cable car) that takes you up and above and through numerous neighborhoods reaching barely You'll watch youngsters playing in the natural pools, hear dogs and roosters sing, and smell that wonderful toasted wood campo perfume, as you soar over schools, houses, beautiful plains, bustling streets, and rivers. There are so many tales of the vistas from above with every swing.

To us tourists, this is a delightful and exhilarating (when it swings out of the station it seems like zip-lining) journey through the northern suburbs of Santo Domingo... for many inhabitants, it's finally a method to go about and connect to new options in the city core. This is a key form of daily local transportation that assists Dominicans and our environment.

11. Museo Fernando Peña Defilló
Museo Fernando Pena Defillo is a magnificent museum and art gallery situated smack dab amid the Colonial Zone. It shows the Peña Defilló family's private collection of Dominican art. It includes a nice outdoor area and rooms with art and literature. A convenient stop between your Zona Colonial tours. the outskirts of La Victoria.

12. Chinatown Sunday Morning Market

Experience a rare mix of Chinese-Dominican culture. Every Sunday, there's a big outdoor market where Chinese and Dominican farmers and street vendors offer great food, beverages, and vegetables cultivated locally.

You may discover Chinese fruits and vegetables growing in the Dominican Republic, frequently stuff that Dominicans have never seen. It's a fantastic experience of two very different cultures coming together. Moreover, you may drop into the various stores and restaurants if you're still hungry or want some particular Asian things to purchase.

13. Los Charcos de Nizao (Day Trip from Santo Domingo) (Day Trip from Santo Domingo)

This epic excursion begins early in the morning, traveling from Santo Domingo. You travel for around two hours to Los Cacaos in the province of San Cristobal. It's classed as an easy trek, but you will get soaked. Within the first 10 minutes of trekking, you'll witness the first emerald green pool. The remainder of the journey (4 hours round trip) consists of magnificent natural ponds enclosed by huge limestone cliffs and mountains.

14. Electric Scooter City Tour

This electric scooter tour allows you to explore as much of La Zona Colonial from the comfort of your scooter. Perfect when you want to discover everything without walking under the blistering hot Caribbean heat. The trip is guided by two Dominican residents and lasts approximately an hour and a half for $20.

15. National Park East (Day Trip) (Day Trip)

National Park East, popularly known as Cotubanama National Park, is approximately two hours from Santo Domingo. This trip takes you into the park's caverns and swimming holes.

It is a pleasant day excursion from Santo Domingo's city life and a terrific approach to discovering our country's eastern natural treasures. If you're headed to Punta Cana following Santo Domingo, this may be a fantastic opportunity to combine a day excursion with transportation! Talk to your guide about it.

16. Parque Mirador Sur

This tiny park is located immediately beneath the Bella Vista area on the posh Anacaona Boulevard. If you prefer an active lifestyle, here is the place to be on a Saturday morning where you can join other Dominican fitness aficionados in jogging, skating, bicycling, and more.

This gorgeous park also features a free outdoor gym as well as fresh coconut water vendors in case you need some refreshment after a long run throughout the park. Parque Mirador Sur is also home to lovely eateries, meadows, a tiny lagoon, and skate/bike rental businesses.

17. Teatro Nacional Eduardo Brito

You won't find visitors in this underappreciated treasure despite it being one of the top spots in Santo Domingo to visit for culture and history! It contains many levels and 3 major venues for all sorts of performances/events such as theatre, ballet, opera, live music, and notable award presentations.

I watched an extremely fascinating play on Ulises Heureaux, one of the Dominican Republic's presidents in the late 1800s.

If you can't get in for a performance, at least attempt to catch a peek of its neoclassical architectural splendor in the gorgeous Plaza de la Cultura.

18. Casa de Teatro

Casa de Teatro is kind of like an arts center in a bohemian-colonial type environment. There is a theatre with an outdoor courtyard and an art gallery beside the entrance. Come here for concerts, performances, theatrical plays, or one of the numerous entertaining neighborhood meet-up activities.

You can see a little bit of everything here. I even went to a geeky Game of Thrones meet-up here and had a blast!

Last time, I also visited their VERY beautiful café upstairs (shown above) but I'm not sure whether it's still open. The upstairs room for art and community gatherings may have been changed into something else.

19. Go Shopping!

Santo Domingo is rich with local artisans who sell their handcrafted items. From artists to jewelry makers and more, make sure you stop into the nooks and crannies of galleries, weekend markets, and other stores to support you. Some of them may be a little more costly since they are distinctive unlike the mass manufactured made-in-China souvenirs. Here are some shops I recommend:

- Nini Cabela's mugs and purses (Afro-heritage influenced) (Afro-heritage inspired)
- Joarla Caridad's larimar and amber jewelry Casa Quien art gallery

20. Museo del Hombre Dominicano

This is the largest Anthropological Museum in Santo Domingo devoted to Dominican culture, heritage, and history. Located in la Plaza de la Cultura in the Gazcue area, it is only a few feet from other significant locations such as the National Theatre, the National Library, the Modern Art Museum, the Natural History Museum, and much more. You'll learn about the island's history, from the Tainos to the Spanish conquest to our African origins.

NOTE: It is mainly closed for refurbishment. We're anxiously waiting for it to reopen entirely!

6 Best Santo Domingo Beaches

In any list of 'Best Vacation Destinations', the Caribbean and its many islands and countries are always certain to feature. The Caribbean Sea has some of the cleanest, warmest, most beautiful seas anywhere on Earth, and the beaches of the numerous islands have the softest sands and nicest temperatures.

A typical Caribbean beach provides perfect conditions for all types of activities from swimming and sunbathing to surfing, snorkeling, water sports, and more. These beaches are the greatest in the world, and the Caribbean offers limitless miles of coastline and hundreds of distinct beaches to pick from.

We suggest that you phone the attractions and restaurants ahead of your visit to check current opening hours.

1. Playa de Guibia
If you're seeking a beach located in Santo Domingo and don't want to have to leave the city to have some fun in the sun, Playa de Guibia is the ideal choice for you.

Situated on the city's major coastal roadway, George Washington Avenue, Playa de Guibia is readily accessible from the central areas and hotels of Santo Domingo.

This beach is highly popular with the locals and livens up in the evenings as people get off work and come down to view the water with their friends and family.

So if you want to enjoy a party environment, make sure to visit Playa de Guibia after the sun has set, but if you prefer a calmer, quieter experience, travel here in the mornings or around noon. It's a modest beach with rocky and sandy parts and great views, as well as convenient access to the bars and restaurants of the city.

2. Playa Boca Chica

If you're staying in Santo Domingo and prepared to go only a little distance for a genuine world-class beach experience, Playa Boca Chica is the spot for you.

It's less than a half-hour drive out of the city and can be accessed through public transit if you don't happen to have a vehicle. Playa Boca Chica is a wide beach with a lot of areas for everyone to enjoy, both on the sand and in the water. Even with all that room, it may still become very busy here since this beach is highly popular with Santo Domingo visitors and locals.

But don't worry, even on the busiest of days, you can always typically find a spare beach umbrella and a few sun loungers to enjoy your time, or you can just stroll farther down the beach to locate a peaceful space on the sand. Either way, when you do find your space on this beach, you'll be able to make the most of its silky white beaches and tranquil, reef-protected seas. Snorkeling, diving, swimming, sunbathing, beach games, and more can all be enjoyed at Playa Boca Chica, and there are several fine bars and restaurants to be found along the edge of the sand as well.

3. Juan Dolio

If Playa Boca Chica is a bit too crowded or has too much of a party scene for you, Juan Dolio is the finest option.

You'll have to be ready to wait a bit longer to enjoy this beach, though, since it is located just under an hour away from Santo Domingo. This distance helps the beach be considerably less busy than the likes of Playa de Guibia and Playa Boca Chica, as many people prefer ease and accessibility and thus don't take the effort to travel out this far. If you are willing to undertake the voyage, you'll be amply rewarded.

Juan Dolio is one of the nicest beaches in the Dominican Republic. Tall, towering coconut trees border the beach, creating wonderful small shaded nooks for people to cool down on the sunniest, hottest days, and there's a lot of room here for people to spread out and not feel crowded at all.

You may just lay back, shut your eyes, and listen to the pleasant murmur of the waves, without having to worry about a single thing. There are several decent restaurants and bars in the neighborhood too, but this is one of the most unspoiled beaches in the Santo Domingo region, so you won't have to worry about music or parties disturbing the tranquil mood.

4. More Info

If you're planning a Caribbean trip, you'll have a lot of different places to select from, and the Dominican Republic is one of the top choices to consider.

It's the most popular destination in the Caribbean, bringing millions of people each year, and the ideal area to base yourself for an entertaining and diverse Dominican Republic holiday in Santo Domingo. Officially called Santo Domingo de Guzmán, Santo Domingo is the capital city of the Dominican Republic and also happens to be the largest metropolis in the entire Caribbean area.

It has a population of roughly 1 million people, with over 2.9 million in the surrounding region.

If you're vacationing in the Santo Domingo region of the Dominican Republic, you'll be delighted to know that some excellent beaches are just a short drive away.

The local coastline is home to some of the nicest beaches in the whole Caribbean, excellent for sunbathing, surfing, snorkeling, swimming, and many other sports. Read through the guide below for vital facts and probable things to do at the top beaches in Santo Domingo.

5. Playa Najayo
Playa Najayo is a prominent beach on the Dominican Republic's Caribbean coast, situated just west of Santo Domingo in the San Cristobal province. Featuring little pebbles and gray sand, this gorgeous beach comprises two separate regions.

One of these beach sections is substantially bigger and includes several bars and restaurants. Playa Najayo is one of the area's most frequented beaches, although it's largely attended by locals. While the seas normally contain powerful waves and smaller stones, there is a little backwater in the middle portion of the beach that's cordoned off from the open ocean by a breakwater.

6. Guayacanes Beach
Guayacanes Beach is situated a little off the usual road in Guayacanes, a tiny fishing community in the Dominican Republic. Locals come to the beach to relax in the turquoise blue seas and enjoy the waves, while fishermen regularly come to the beach as they go out into the sea and return.

The beach boasts a white sand beach that's extremely attractive and perfect for an easy walk during dawn or to relax and watch the sunset at the end of the day. Guests must wear appropriate water shoes owing to certain portions of Guayacanes Beach being rocky.

How to Save Money in Santo Domingo

Learn how to haggle Store pricing is established, while the price of just about anything from a street seller is negotiable. Learn to say, "Gracias no, pero es demasiado caro," (No thanks, but too pricey) and see how much lower they're willing to go.

Skip the colonial tour There will be dozens of young males loitering about the Zona Colonial wanting to tour you around. Invest in an excellent city map and explore (for free) on your own.

Visit aboard a cruise ship You could spend a few days seeing Santo Domingo, or you could catch the highlights in a six-hour port of call and save on flight and accommodation expenses.

What You Need to Know

There's lots of top-notch shopping

From amber and larimar (Dominican turquoise) jewelry to hand-wrapped cigars, the DR as a whole is noted for its high-quality souvenirs. You'll find stalls and businesses everywhere along the Malecón and throughout the Zona Colonial.

The nightlife is fantastic

Even the hotel clubs are very busy in Santo Domingo. And you'll also discover an incredible choice of pubs, dance clubs, and casinos along the Malecón.

Béisbol is the sport of choice

Several big league baseball stars got their "swinging" start in this city: The Pittsburgh Pirates' Pedro Alvarez, the Colorado Rockies' Cristhian Adames, and the Boston Red Sox's David Ortiz, to mention a few. Go cheered for tomorrow's MLB players at the Estadio Quisqueya.

Culture & Customs

Although many shops do take U.S. dollars in Santo Domingo, the national currency (which is also the one most widely used) is the Dominican peso. The currency rate changes from time to time, but $1 normally equals around RD$45.41. To avoid expensive conversion rates at hotels and airport kiosks, try converting some money via your bank before leaving the U.S.

Also bear in mind that tipping in the Dominican Republic is a little different than it is in the U.S. In Santo Domingo and other Dominican cities, a 10 percent gratuity is automatically included in restaurant invoices. But if you believe you had great treatment, it is traditional to provide an extra 10 percent tip. As for taxi drivers, gratuities are not frequently offered (although tips for outstanding service will not be turned down) (but tips for great service will not be turned down).

Those who intend on visiting Santo Domingo should also be informed of the Dominican Republic's admission procedures. American travelers visiting the nation for 30 days or less are not needed to apply for a visa.

However, upon arrival, Americans are required to pay a $10 charge for a tourist card (in addition to possessing a valid passport) (in addition to bringing a valid passport). For the latest admission criteria and travel recommendations, check out the Embassy of the Dominican Republic in the United States website.

10 Great Restaurants in Santo Domingo

These fantastic eateries in Santo Domingo are staples in the city's ever-evolving culinary scene. Dominican cuisine is a fantastic collision of flavors from throughout the globe, with influences that range from Spain to Africa. To enjoy some of the country's very finest restaurants, you won't be shocked to find that the city of Santo Domingo is overflowing with possibilities.

Whether you want to enjoy traditional cuisine that explores local flavors or an elaborate feast that exhibits a global viewpoint, there's no lack of world-class restaurants to consider. Here, we showcase some of the most known venues for when you want to sample the greatest offers from Santo Domingo's chefs.

1. El Mesón de la Cava
Exceptional Caribbean and French cuisines in an imaginative setting

Good for: Food

Dinner at El Mesón de la Cava is surely a unique experience for those visiting Santo Domingo. Opened in 1967, this long-standing tradition sees Caribbean and French-inspired meals served within the depths of a natural limestone cave.

On the menu, you'll find everything from wood-grilled octopus and Monterrey chicken breast to seafood paella.

Accompanying your meal is a wide wine selection that brings together extraordinary wines from local and international vineyards. Throughout El Mesón de la Cava's different rooms, including a lovely outdoor patio, you'll come across a vast selection of real artifacts left behind by pirates and guerilla fighters.

Location: Av. Mirador Sur 1, Santo Domingo 00000, Dominican Republic
Open: Daily from 11.30 am until 11 pm
Phone: +1 809-533-2818

2. Laurel Incredible good dining without the hefty price tag

Good for: Food
Laurel is well known as one of Santo Domingo's premier fine-dining establishments. Providing tourists with a world-class culinary experience that doesn't seem unduly tense, it's the perfect setting for a luxurious but relaxing lunch or supper with your loved ones.

Renowned for its pleasant environment and exceptional service, customers are spoiled for choice when deciding on something to eat.

With a broad range of choices on the menu, including seafood, pizzas, and salads, there's also a selection of vegan and vegetarian dishes to guarantee there's something for everyone. To start, choose the Memphis Nachos, while ginger- and soy-glazed fish and the classic Laurel burger are superb mains.
Location: Calle Andrés Julio Aybar, Santo Domingo, Dominican Republic

Open: Friday–Saturday from noon to 1 am, Sunday–Thursday from midday to midnight
Phone: +1 809-908-0200

3. Buche Perico
Fresh Caribbean meals surrounded by greenery

Good for: Food
Bucho Perico helps customers feel like they haven't left behind the Dominican Republic's gorgeous scenery.

Situated in the historic area of Ciudad Colonial, luxuriant plants spread from the soaring glass roof to the floor. There's also an inside waterfall to enhance the restaurant's tropical feel.

Having located in a sufficiently secluded area, you'll be served a polished Caribbean menu including a multitude of tasty delicacies. Ranging from fresh tuna and ripe banana ravioli to shrimp pasta and pork ribs, you won't be disappointed when the plates arrive.

There's also a great wine selection showcasing award-winning wines from throughout the world.
Location: Calle El Conde 53, Santo Domingo 10210, Dominican Republic

Open: Monday–Friday from 11 am to 9 pm, Saturday–Sunday from 9 am to 7 pm
Phone: +1 809-475-6451

4. Pat'e Palo Meaty feasts cooked to perfection in a historic locale

Good for: Food
Pat'e Palo is certainly one of the most popular restaurants in Santo Domingo, recognized for its refined European-style food and cozy tavern environment. With the structure going back over 500 years and touted as the earliest bar in the Americas, you'll find sights such as Alcazar de Colón and Columbus Park within close vicinity.

There are 3 different locations at Pat'e Palo — the main restaurant, the bar, and the terrace. Here, you may experience staples like beef ribeye, fire-roasted pork ribs, or traditional mashed plantains. With Pat'e Palo available for breakfast, lunch, and supper, go along and sample unmatched flavors any time of the day.
Location: Plaza Espana, Santo Domingo 10210, Dominican Republic

Open: Daily from 11.30 am till 1 am
Phone: +1 809-687-8089

5. Don Pepe
The city's greatest seafood for over 30 years

Good for: Food
Don Pepe is the place to be in Santo Domingo when you're wanting top-notch Spanish food. Situated in the upscale suburb of Piantini, this opulent setting is mirrored in the restaurant itself, with magnificent furnishings and imaginative foods on the

menu. Having opened its doors more than 30 years ago, Don Pepe is a go-to location for travelers in quest of the city's greatest delicacies.

For aficionados of grilled and seafood delicacies, ensure this establishment is high on your dining shortlist. There are magnificent lamb chops and suckling pigs, among classic tapas such as arroz con calamares (Spanish rice with squid) and arroz con pollo (Spanish rice with chicken) (Spanish rice with chicken).

With a red wine selection including over 500 bottles from Spain's greatest areas, supper is certain to be spectacular at Don Pepe.
Location: Calle Porfirio Herrera 31, Santo Domingo, Dominican Republic

Open: Daily from lunchtime to midnight
Phone: +1 809-563-4440

6. Jalao

Enjoy exceptional eating, dancing, and live music

Good for:FoodNightlife

Jalao is where residents and visitors come to discover lively Dominican culture. Spread in a big area, this much-loved restaurant offers 5 separate bars and a giant stage so you can dance the night away in style.

With classic Dominican features covering practically every surface, Jalao is a tremendously popular destination for a reason.

Alongside its vibrant, tropical-inspired décor, the cuisine is equally as amazing. To start, yucca flower empanadas are a terrific option before plunging into mains such as homemade gnocchi, Dominican stew, spicy red wine oxtail, and pork ribs. For a colorful night filled with local cuisine, dancing, and live music, don't miss your opportunity to experience Jalao.

Location: Calle el Conde, Ciudad Colonial, Santo Domingo 10210, Dominican Republic

Open: Monday–Friday from 6 pm to 2 am, Saturday–Sunday from 12 pm to 2 am
Phone: +1 809-792-1262

7. El Conuco
Live music and traditional Dominican foods are certain to impress

Good for: FoodNightlife
El Conuco is perfect for experiencing the Dominican Republic's legendary hospitality since you'll be treated to delicious cuisine and entertainment as soon as you walk inside. Although it's on the more touristic side of eateries in Santo Domingo, it doesn't mean the tastes on the show aren't as real as everywhere else in the city.

You'll discover a superb assortment of tacos stuffed with Dominican-style beef, goat stew, or roasted pig ribs. There are also excellent seafood alternatives, such as cod cooked with Creole flavors and Atlantic shrimp served with mango and dates. As you enjoy your dinner, amazing merengue and bachata performers will keep you delighted late into the evening.
Location: Calle Casimiro de Moya #152, Santo Domingo, Dominican Republic

Open: Daily from 11.30 am to midnight
Phone: +1 809-686-0129

8. Aubergine

Escape the city for European-inspired food and amazing vistas

Good for: Food

Aubergine may not be situated inside the borders of Santo Domingo, but it's surely worth a trek into the hills. Situated in the little village of La Colonia, amid the San Cristóbal mountains, this beautiful restaurant provides first-rate meals and breathtaking rural views from a tall patio.

Drawing on culinary ideas from around Europe, Aubergine provides a significant contrast from many other restaurants in town. Highlights on the menu include fish with ricotta cheese, mozzarella chicken breast, and the restaurant's contemporary twist on sushi. For a refreshing treat that fills off your overall dining experience, try the avocado ice cream.

Location: Paseo del Manantial KM 6, Cambita Garabitos 91000, Dominican Republic

Open: Friday–Sunday from lunchtime to 6 pm (closed Mondays to Thursdays) (closed Mondays to Thursdays)
Phone: +1 809-729-9364

9. La Briciola de Santo Domingo
Cuisine and ambiance best enjoyed with friends and family

Good for: FoodNightlife

La Briciola de Santo Domingo is an excellent site for when you wish to enjoy the romanticism of Santo Domingo. First founded in 1994 in a lively section of the city, the Italian and Mediterranean food on exhibit guarantees the restaurant has remained a popular destination throughout the following years. Alongside frequent jazz performances and live pianists, supper is often a romantic occasion.

With numerous elegant open-air eating places surrounded by plants and Spanish décor, spending a night here with your best friends will make a memorable memory.

La Briciola de Santo Domingo keeps visitors coming back for more with its broad menu of handmade pasta and seafood staples.
Location: Calle Arzobispo Meriño 152A, Santo Domingo 10210, Dominican Republic

Open: Monday–Saturday from lunchtime to midnight, Sunday from midday to 6 pm
Phone: +1 829-719-2078

10. SBG Sophia's Bar & Grill

Glamorous dinner with powerful drinks and delicious foreign platters

Good for: Food

Nightlife

Sophia's Bar & Grill is nestled in a hip suburb amid Santo Domingo's famous sites. The restaurant's décor blends leather seats, dark wood accents, and towering pillars to provide an undoubtedly elegant feel. Its menu caters to worldwide tastes, featuring dishes drawn from cuisines from throughout the globe.

While luscious grilled foods are a highlight, customers at Sophia's Bar & Grill will also discover exquisite carpaccio and an imaginative sushi bar.

You may also enjoy some of the greatest cocktails in town, with a choice of distinctive beverages carrying a huge punch.
Location: Calle Paseo de los Locutores 9, Santo Domingo 10149, Dominican Republic

Open: Monday–Friday from lunchtime to 9 pm, Saturday–Sunday from midday to 7 pm
Phone: +1 809-620-1001

Getting Around Santo Domingo

PUBLIC TRANSPORTATION

The Dominican Republic's public transportation infrastructure is surprisingly contemporary and vast. Dominicans are continually on the road–visiting relatives in the countryside, doing business, or trudging to school.

Taxis are widespread, Uber is accessible in three main cities–Santo Domingo, Santiago, and Puerto Plata–and there's always a type of bus service, large or tiny, traveling to whatever town or city you choose to visit. Aside from being the cheapest way to travel, public transportation is a terrific opportunity to glimpse everyday life in the DR and is certain to be a memorable experience.

SANTO DOMINGO SUBWAY

Metro Santo Domingo runs two lines, largely utilized by citizens going to work. But there are many stations near the sites. Line 1 travels north to south along Máximo Gómez Avenue, from the Villa Mella region all the way to Centro de los Héroes, where Congress, the Supreme Court of Justice, and the Department of Migration, among other government buildings, are situated.

The Casandra Damirón station on Line 1 takes you straight inside Plaza de la Cultura, home of significant institutions and the National Theater. Line 2 goes east to west on John F. Kennedy Avenue, passing via Ágora Mall at the Pedro Mir station, and the Felix Sánchez Olympic Stadium.

A roundtrip subway price costs RD$15 for a rechargeable metro card, plus RD$40 roundtrip, or RD$80 for a day pass. The subway runs every day from 6 am-10:30 pm.

Taxis are readily accessible in big cities and towns, frequently stationed outside major bus terminals, or hotel and tourist zones. In the main cities like Santo Domingo, Santiago, and Puerto Plata, your best chance is to contact one of the major 24-hour taxi service companies–ask your hotel or a local for the best ones, and to make the call for you. In Santo Domingo, for instance, Apolo Taxi is popular, as is Aero Taxi.

When contacting, ask the taxi phone operator to confirm the color of the vehicle and the projected wait time. You should also ask for confirmation of the fee to your location –rates inside cities are regulated by the taxi organization.

UBER & CABIFY

The prominent ridesharing app service UBER began in the Dominican Republic in 2015 and is presently operating in three main cities: Santo Domingo, Santiago, and Puerto Plata. Cabify also operates in Santo Domingo.

These applications are as safe to use in the DR as in any other place. More guests are turning to them because of the language barrier—no need to talk to a cab operator on the phone. The vehicles are also generally in superior condition, with functional seatbelts and air-conditioning, in addition to decreased fees when there is no high traffic.

LONG DISTANCE LOCAL TRAVEL INTERURBAN COACH BUS SERVICE

One of the primary attractions of the DR is the easy, economical huge coach bus services linking the various locations in the nation. Three dependable firms are offering daily service to key hubs, in contemporary, air-conditioned buses with Wi-Fi and entertainment.

Metro Tours buses link Santo Domingo, Santiago, Puerto Plata, Sosúa, La Romana/Casa de Campo, and there are daily departures to Port-au-Prince, Haiti. Caribe Tours services Santo Domingo, Santiago, Puerto Plata, and Sosúa –with more frequent daily departures–Barahona, Cabrera, Jarabacoa, La Vega, Montecristi, Samaná, and other places in the Dominican Republic, as well as Haiti. Expreso Bávaro is the sole significant bus service linking Santo Domingo and Bávaro every day, suitable for Punta Cana vacationers.

Bus tickets vary from RD$200-RD$500 one-way. Make sure to arrive at least one hour before departure to assure sitting space, and carry a sturdy jacket or scarf with you on board, since these buses prefer to maintain the air-conditioning at its lowest position.

LOW-COST MINIVAN BUS SERVICE OR GAUGES

Smaller, privately-owned and operated minivan buses called guaguas travel planned routes daily, bringing tourists inside a city, or long-distance to small and big locations across the Dominican Republic.

The long-distance guaguas are equally as luxurious as the giant coach buses, seating no more than 20-25 people, each with a dedicated seat and enabling Wi-Fi connectivity. Look out for the ones branded "Expreso" to your destination–they don't stop along the route to pick up people, unlike the ordinary ones, which shortens your journey.

IN-CITY TRANSPORTATION\sMINIVAN BUSES

The inner-city guaguas tend to be white vans, stopping to pick up or drop off anybody along the prescribed route as many times as it takes, and are the slowest means of traveling. Passengers are squeezed in, and room arises miraculously just when you think there isn't any left.

It's also the cheapest option to travel inside a city or municipal borders. Be careful to take a tiny change for the fare, since these vans don't carry much cash—you might be left paying extra otherwise. Each guagua has a driver, and a conductor who shouts out for passengers along the route, manages to collect fares, and hollers out desired stops to the driver. Inform the conductor of your destination as soon as you board, and are ready to pay straight away or as soon as required.

MOTORBIKE TAXIS OR MOTORCOACHES

Motorbike taxis are popular among residents in major cities like Santo Domingo or Puerto Plata, and even Jarabacoa since they are the cheapest and quickest method to get through traffic. But this is also the most hazardous method to commute, especially in cities or regions with high traffic.

Many motorcycle taxis don't supply helmets, while they are legally obligated to do so. Riding a leisurely bike taxi through the mountain villages of Jarabacoa and Constanza, though, is a terrific way to take in the stunning view. The official motorcycle taxis normally wear a vest of neon color, however, notice that that is not always the case. Ask for the moto concho hub in your town, or receive a suggestion from your hotel. Fares vary from RD$25 to RD$75 in-city, depending on the distance.

SHARED TAXIS OR CONCHOS
Also called carrier–conchos, carritos, or simply conchos, these four-door sedans are shared taxis, comparable to the in-city guaguas since they follow certain routes and stop wherever on the route as desired by customers. You may find them in large cities, as well as in towns and villages.

They are a little more comfortable than the guagua, although people are also crowded in at the rear and the front. Fares vary from RD$25-50 depending on the distance–significantly lower than a private taxi cost, which begins at RD$150.

HIGHWAYS

The Dominican Republic is well-serviced by extensive, modern roadways connecting its main towns and coasts, and interconnecting the most popular tourist attractions. In excellent shape, they expose the country's spectacular scenery, notably along the routes from Santo Domingo to the Samaná Peninsula or Jarabacoa, and along the coast of Puerto Plata.

Familiarize yourself with these five main highways–particularly if you intend on hiring a vehicle and touring the country's numerous regions. Expect tolls, depending on your origin and destination–inquire at your guesthouse before commencing your journey. For instance, the roadway from Santo Domingo to Boca Chica contains a single tollbooth, whereas there are four from Santo Domingo to Bávaro. Toll prices vary, ranging from RD$60 to RD$100 for each booth. Carry small changes in Dominican pesos. Dollars are accepted, but any applicable change will be in the local currency.

Route 1: Autopista Duarte – Santo Domingo to Santiago: The Duarte Highway is a divided four-lane highway linking the north and south of the Dominican Republic. It's a two-hour scenic drive from the capital up to the second largest city of Santiago, also leading towards Jarabacoa and La Vega.

Route 3: Autopista Las Américas: This highway links Santo Domingo's Las Américas International Airport with the city of Santo Domingo going west, or to the beach town of Boca Chica going east. It eventually meets with the Autopista Coral towards La Romana.

Route 3: Autopista Oscar de la Renta: This highway, also known as Autopista del Coral, links Santo Domingo with the Punta Cana resort area, bypassing Higüey, in less than three hours, and reaches La Romana in less than one hour.

Route 5: Carretera de Puerto Plata: This two-lane highway runs along the North Coast in one of the most colorful, quaint drives in the country. It runs by fishing communities, beaches, distant beautiful hills, and everyday campo life.

Route 7: Santo Domingo to Samaná Highway: Route 7 connects Santo Domingo with the northern Samaná Peninsula.

The vistas on Route 7 are exceptional, with lush coconut tree-punctuated slopes from a coconut oil farm, rising above a vivid blue sea. Another option is to reach Las Terrenas via the Boulevard Turístico del Atlántico or Route 133, worth the extra US$11 in toll costs for its stunning, meandering coastline vistas, and a panoramic viewing point over the Bay of Cosón.

Plan Your Dominican Republic Honeymoon

The Dominican Republic is a favorite honeymoon destination because of everything that the lovely island can offer at a fair price. Whether you're searching for exciting activities and adventure, long days lazing by the seaside, or a combination of all, honeymooners will find it in the DR.

With its sandy gorgeous beaches, a myriad of inexpensive resorts, and magnificent natural beauty, the DR is a honeymooner's delight. Looking for a honeymoon that's remote, tropical, and full of action and relaxation? This is the one.

When to honeymoon in the Dominican Republic

The greatest time of the year to visit the Dominican Republic is between March and May. The peak season rush will be easing down and the weather is still wonderful. It keeps warm year-round in the DR with highs that average approximately 80 degrees. But, hurricane season is something to keep in mind.

It lasts from June and November and the DR does have a history of seeing some destructive tropic storms in the past, with September and October being the most active months.

Things to do on your Honeymoon Walk La Plaza:

This magnificent swimming area located outside of Punta Cana is a terrific spot to hike. Their crystal-clear waters, many waterfalls, and entertaining adventure will make newlyweds feel like they're in another universe. Guided trips to hike La Plaza should be high on every honeymooner's itinerary.

Caribbean Water Sports Activities: There are so many enjoyable things to do in the water. The DR provides a plethora of water activities including kayaking, snorkeling, stand-up paddle boarding, scuba diving, catamaran sailing, and deep-sea fishing.

The DR is recognized for its deep sea and big game fishing. Try to capture a marlin, yellowfin tuna, or even a barracuda while you're out on the sea. Aside from that, there are lots of colorful fish and undersea sea caves to explore as well.

Hit the Beach: Probably one of the greatest reasons why any honeymooners come to the Dominican Republic is for their famed beaches. The cerulean blue ocean and beautiful sandy beaches constitute a romantic paradise. Plus, there are lots of beaches. The Punta Cana/Bavaro beaches are more than 20 miles long and on the Sama Peninsula, the famed Playa Rincon is one of the most gorgeous beaches on the earth.

World Class Golf: The DR is a favorite place for golfers who enjoy the game and attractive courses. The weather year-round is fantastic and the shifting landscape of the island which includes hills, coasts, and an abundance of A+ courses is a magnet to visitors and honeymooners from all over the globe.

Horseback Riding: This is a classic honeymoon favorite of couples visiting the Dominican Republic. Depending on where you are, there are different timetables to select from. Horseback riding on the beach at sunset seems quite romantic. Or if you don't want to ride on sand, consider an inner track past waterfalls, up and down slopes, or through the forest.

Whale Watching: Did you know apart from Hawaii, the Dominican Republic is regarded as one of the greatest sites in the world to observe whales? Honeymooners who like to go out on the open ocean will appreciate this activity since humpbacks migrate to the DR to mate and give birth so your chances of sighting one, depending on what time of the year you go, are high. Check out Samana Bay for booking options.

Exploring Samana: Speaking of Samana, it offers a lot more than whale viewing to offer honeymooners. The Samana Peninsula juts out slightly east of the nation and contains hills that run down the center, a seashore on either side, and the magnificent coastal town of Samana. The ocean is warmer here and wandering lonely, uninhabited beaches is also a terrific exercise.

Where to go in the Dominican Republic
Punta Cana

The fabled Punta Cana, one of the most popular destinations for honeymooners to travel in all of the Dominican Republic, lives up to its reputation.

The white sandy beaches are nearly so lovely you wouldn't believe they're genuine. It'll be uncommon that newlyweds won't want to be on the beach, but when they retreat to their rooms, they'll have much to select from.

Punta Cana is all-inclusive resort bliss and we've selected some of our favorites in the area below. Punta Cana is a popular honeymoon location due to its magnificent views, luxurious resorts, and ability to help couples relax.

Santo Domingo
This bustling and flourishing town is the capital of the Dominican Republic and is worth experiencing. It's also one of the biggest cities in the Caribbean by population.

If you're searching for a little nightlife, a whole lot of adventure, and someplace fresh and fascinating to discover, the capital city of Santo Domingo is great for your honeymoon. There's lots to do, plenty to see, and plenty to eat. Fun activities like merengue dancing, romantic meals, and cultural excursions await the newlyweds who desire to visit Santo Domingo.

La Romana

The picturesque coast side city of La Romana is great for honeymooners who are trying to escape the hustle and the bustle. Their gorgeous beaches set against a Dominican Republic sunset are one of the most romantic vistas couples can experience. Plus, the population of the town is limited, so if you're searching for a tough trip across the coastlines and valleys of the Dominican Republic, La Romana is the place to be.

Much to many husband's joy. It's also a golfer's heaven. World-renowned golfers prefer to play at Casa De Campo. Beyond golfing, La Romana has excellent seas for swimming and snorkeling, and attractive art museums and galleries for honeymooners who wish to explore the historical side of the city.

Ultimate Luxury Camping Getaway for Two on Heavenly Playa Rincon, Dominican Republic

These gorgeous glamping tents on the beach of Playa Rincon are great for honeymooners who are wishing to be in nature but are not entirely exposed to it. The jacuzzi pools and facilities that come along with the glamping tents are romantic and appropriate for a honeymoon retreat.

Lovely Beachside Vacation Rental with a Jet Tub in Las Terrenas, Dominican Republic
This gorgeous oceanfront property is excellent for honeymooners who are searching for lots of space and quiet. The sophisticated and elegant facilities together with the peaceful villa will enable newlyweds to appreciate the property and each other.

SANTO DOMINGO, DOMINICAN REPUBLIC

The Historic Hodelpa Nicolas de Ovando Hotel
This premium boutique hotel provides honeymooners with the ideal home base while they explore Santo Domingo. The gorgeous property is serene and has 92 rooms.

Their wonderful restaurant is widely commended and the property is formed of three stone homes erected in 1502 and is the rebuilt 16th-century residence of the city's founder, Nicolás de Ovando, the first governor of the Americas.

Casa Bonita Santo Domingo
This magnificent all-inclusive facility is great for honeymooners who prefer adventure and leisure. Casa Bonita provides a peaceful and romantic spa, a stunning infinity pool, a hot tub, rooms with rain

showers, and a wonderful view of the Caribbean. Their amazing facilities also include internet, breakfast, ziplining, horseback riding, snorkeling, and bike rentals. The stunning backdrop of the hotel is a perfect site for honeymooners to feel amorous while all of their complimentary activities are certain to bring honeymooners out of their rooms and into some fun.

Puntacana Resort & Club
This is a beautiful location situated in Punta Cana, Dominican Republic where couples may go for a romantic beachside holiday. The Puntacana Resort & Club is more than simply a resort and club.

This luxurious hotel is made up of 13 oceanfront private villas that are meant for honeymooners. In addition, honeymooners can enjoy a serene and peaceful day at the Six Senses Spa, the only location within the Americas, which provides an array of different treatments, specifically for couples such as the Romance Journey ritual, including a full body massage and facial specifically formulated for each individual.

For honeymooners who are seeking something more active, enjoy the two 18-hole golf courses situated inside the resort, Corales Golf Course, home to the only PGA tour stop in the Dominican Republic. Honeymooners may also enjoy supper at one of the nine restaurants available inside the resort, including two AAA Diamond Award-winning diners.

Majestic Elegance Punta Cana

This stunning seaside resort is one of Punta Cana's newest and most luxurious all-inclusive resorts. The 600-room hotel boasts a big pool, a stunning white-sand beach, seven restaurants, and a name-brand liquor for no additional fee. If you're searching for intimacy and luxury on your honeymoon, the Majestic Elegance Punta Cana is the place to stay. The resort contains an adult-only part that offers access to exclusive pool areas, beachfront rooftop bars, VIP lounges, 24-hour room service, an in-room bar selection, and 13 bars placed around the property.

Sanctuary Cap Cana, Punta Cana, Dominican republic
This gorgeous resort recently went through a multimillion-dollar refurbishment. The adult-only facility boasts brand new, luxurious rooms appropriate for queens and kings celebrating their marriage, including the Castle Island Suite that treats guests to the solitude of access to their island.

With amenities with breathtaking views of the Caribbean Sea, date locations at the resort's gourmet dining outlets, and a world-class spa with a variety of romantic couples treatments and a new ZEN garden, shower trails, and hydrotherapeutic pools. The resort is centered on a colonial Spanish vibe and situated on more than 20 acres with 2,100 feet of pure coastline.

Casa de Campo
Located in the Dominican Republic, the Casa de Campo is a well-known resort for romance and honeymoons. Their excellent meals and superb wines, a 370-slip Marina & Yacht Club, Polo & Equestrian Club, La Terraza Tennis Center, and 245-acre Shooting Club are a few of the most spectacular attractions.

Spanning 7,000 lush acres on the southern coast of the Dominican Republic, this luxurious Caribbean. The whole site is a hamlet designed like a 16th-century Mediterranean city with boutique stores, museums, and a 5,000-seat Grecian-style amphitheater opened by Frank Sinatra in August of 1982. They also provide a year-round Romance in the Air package that includes Dominican-born Aphrodisiac – Mamajuana. This drink was previously utilized as a vitality drink and was only accessible "underground."

CHIC by Royalton — Punta Cana, Dominican Republic

CHIC by Royalton: This facility offers newlyweds an All Exclusive™ with a fantastic poolside setting. From midday parties to nighttime-themed parties and exciting performances, CHIC is a perfect honeymoon place for couples who are eager to party.

With 320 elegant apartments on the resort, six distinct restaurants, and various bars, newlyweds will have enough luxury to keep them occupied.

The honeymoon package includes a free hydrotherapy circuit at the Spa, a newlywed room upgrade, and a romantic supper for two on the beach. For a truly elevated honeymoon experience, CHIC couples have the chance to upgrade to Diamond Club™ where they can check in to their lobby, relax in their lounge complete with complimentary snacks and top-shelf beverages and enjoy indulgences such as personal butlers, private mermaid pool, and an exclusive beach area. The bottom level of Diamond Club™ suites is embellished with personal plunge pools that serve as the ideal area to soak in all the excitement poolside while resting waist-deep in calm waters away from the throng.

Barceló Bávaro Beach: Punta Cana
The adults-only, all-inclusive resort is situated along Bavaro Beach with 580 rooms, 11 restaurants, two bars, and a big swimming pool. Honeymooners will undoubtedly have enough to keep them amused on this property.

The resort's Premium Level Ocean Front Suite Area is perfect for honeymooners since it comes with a hot tub, a sitting room, and breathtaking views of the Caribbean. Plus, visitors enjoy a free round of golf per person and Premium Level privileges (including concierge service, 24-hour room service, and unlimited daily use of the U-Spa's hydrotherapy circuit).

The resort's free 'In Love Package,' comprises an upgrade to the next hotel category, priority check-in, late check-out, continental breakfast in the room on the first day, and a bottle of sparkling wine and Petit Fours delivered to the room. Aside from all these attractions, there's also a nightclub, a casino, and a state-of-the-art health and wellness center. This romantic and adventurous hotel was created for honeymooners.

Zoetry Agua Punta Cana
With 96 magnificent rooms, lovely gardens, an outdoor pool, a spa, a fitness center, four gourmet restaurants, three bars and lounges, room service, and free WiFi, this facility offers everything that newlyweds will need for a romantic holiday. This is one of the top-rated hotels in Punta Cana because

the exquisite rooms include hardwood flooring, palapa roofs, huge flat-screen TVs, and private balconies with fantastic views of the gardens or the sea. The minibars are refilled twice a day and Zoetry Agua Punta Cana is specially created for newlyweds who desire luxury, relaxation, and romance.

Is a honeymoon in the Dominican Republic safe?

Yes. The Dominican Republic is safe to go to. While the island's name has periodically visited news sources regarding murder or theft, over the last few years, the country's homicide rate has plummeted. In 2012, the rates were 22.1 per 100,000 individuals and their rates have since reduced to 10.4 in 2018.

How to be safe in the Dominican Republic

While the Dominican Republic is safe to go to, like any form of travel, whether local or international, it's always wise to keep careful. Below are a few strategies to make sure you make it back home with your goods in tow.

Resort: Resorts around the DR are a dime a dozen and always have tight security. The possibilities of criminality inside a resort are relatively minimal. These are possibilities to climb when travelers come to the city, particularly alone and especially at night. Explore the city, but do it right:

Go in a group or with another person to experience everything that the Dominican Republic has to offer outside the resort for honeymooners. And be careful not to be in remote locations, such as parks at night or alone.

Travel light: When you're in the city, be sure to store your valuables and anything you don't want to be taken back in the hotel safe.

If there's a problem: Call hotel security or the police to report the incident.

Conclusion

The Dominican Republic is one of the best countries you'll ever dream of visiting.

"Good luck on your Trip to The Dominican Republic"

Printed in Great Britain
by Amazon